Watch It Grow

Life Cycles

Siân Smith

www.heinemannraintree.com
Visit our website to find out more information about Heinemann-Raintree books.

To order:

☎ Phone 888-454-2279

🖳 Visit www.heinemannraintree.com to browse our catalog and order online.

© 2012 Heinemann Library
an imprint of Capstone Global Library, LLC
Chicago, Illinois

Customer Service: 888-454-2279
Visit our website at www.heinemannraintree.com

Edited by Rebecca Rissman, Daniel Nunn, and Harriet Milles
Designed by Joanna Hinton-Malivoire
Picture research by Mica Brancic
Originated by Capstone Global Library Ltd.
Production by Eirian Griffiths
Printed and bound in China by Leo Paper Products Ltd

15 14 13 12 11
10 9 8 7 6 5 4 3 2 1

Library of Congress Cataloging-in-Publication Data
Smith, Siân.
 Life cycles / Sian Smith.
   p. cm.
 Includes bibliographical references and index.
 ISBN 978-1-4329-5351-5 (hc)—ISBN 978-1-4329-5496-3 (pb) 1. Life cycles (Biology) I. Title.
 QH501.S56 2012
 571.8—dc22   2010044795

Acknowledgments
The author and publishers are grateful to the following for permission to reproduce copyright material: Photolibrary **p. 16** (Animals Animals/Zigmund Leszczynski); Shutterstock **pp. 4 bottom left** (© Antos777), **4 bottom middle** (© Natalie Jean), **4 bottom right** (© Geanina Bechea), **4 top left** (© B. Stefanov), **4 top middle** (© Stephanie Barbary), **4 top right** (© Trucic), **5 top left** (© Joy Brown), **5 top right** (© Outsider), **5 bottom left** (© Alexnika), **5 bottom right** (© Natalia Yudenich), **6** (© Bluerain), **7** (© Bogdan Wankowicz), **8** (© S-eyerkaufer), **9 left** (© Triff), **9 right** (© Jan Zoetekouw), **10** (© Stargazer), **11 top left** (© Orionmystery@flickr), **11 top right** (© Yellowj), **11 bottom left** (© Ann Worthy), **11 bottom right** (© Eric Isselée), **12** (© Seleznev Valery), **13** (© Koshevnyk), **14** (© Greg Henry), **15** (© Alexander Chelmodeev), **17** (© Cathy Keifer), **18** (© Petrov Anton), **19 top left** (© Splash), **19 top right** (© Jan van der Hoeven), **19 bottom left** (© Torsten Dietrich), **19 bottom right** (© Dr. Morley Read, **20 top left** (© Melissa King), **20 top right** (© Ivan Pavlisko), **20 bottom left** (© Privilege), **20 bottom middle & bottom right** (© Yuri Arcurs), **21 left** (© rSnapshotPhotos), **21 right** (© Monkey Business Images), **22 top left** (© Marta P.), **22 top middle** (© Leolintang), **22 top right** (© Shane W Thompson), **22 bottom left** (© Olga Lipatova), **22 bottom middle** (© Pichugin Dmitry), **22 bottom right** (© Liew Weng Keong).

Front cover photograph reproduced with permission of Photolibrary (Stockbroker); back cover photograph Shutterstock (© Jan Zoetekouw).

We would like to thank Michael Bright for his invaluable help in the preparation of this book.

Every effort has been made to contact copyright holders of any material reproduced in this book. Any omissions will be rectified in subsequent printings if notice is given to the publisher.

Some words appear in bold, **like this**. You can find out what they mean in "Words to Know" on page 23.

Contents

About this series

Books in this series introduce readers to the life cycle of different plants and animals. Use this book to stimulate discussion about how all living things have life cycles and how some life cycles are similar, while others are very different.

What Is a Life Cycle?

There are many different types of living things. All animals, such as birds, insects, and people are living things. All plants are living things, too. All living things have a life cycle.

A life cycle shows the changes, or different **stages**, that a living thing goes through in its life. These changes follow a **pattern**. They happen in the same order for each living thing.

Life Begins

The main **stages** in a life cycle are the same for all living things. The start of a life cycle is when life begins. An animal life cycle might start with an egg or a baby.

first leaves

shoot

seed

root

For most plants, life begins with a seed. When a seed has water and sunlight, it can begin to grow into a plant.

Growing Up

Baby animals grow up to become adults who can care for themselves. Animals and plants go through lots of different changes before they become adults.

Some living things take a long time to grow up. Others grow up quickly. A sunflower seed can become a fully grown plant in about 12 weeks. It takes an elephant many years to become an adult.

Making New Life

When animals become adults they can create new life by making babies. This is called **reproduction**. Plants make new plants by reproducing, too.

ladybug **larva**

Some animals start life inside their mother's body. Some animals start life in eggs. Some baby animals look very different from their parents at first. Others look just like their parents.

pollen

Most plants make new life with seeds. To make a seed, **pollen** has to get from one part of a flower to another. Pollen can be carried by the wind, or by insects, birds, and bats.

seed

Once a flower has the pollen it needs, a seed starts to grow inside the flower. Seeds have cases around them to keep them safe. Inside each seed is the start of a new plant.

Dying

Nothing that is living can stay alive forever. After time, all living things will get old and die. This is part of the life cycle, too.

young tree

Dying is the last **stage** in a life cycle. But life cycles go on because animals make babies and plants make seeds. This starts the life cycle all over again.

Unusual Life Cycles

old skin

Many animals go through amazing changes to become adults. Some animals grow new skin. They lose their old skin as they grow up. This is called **molting**.

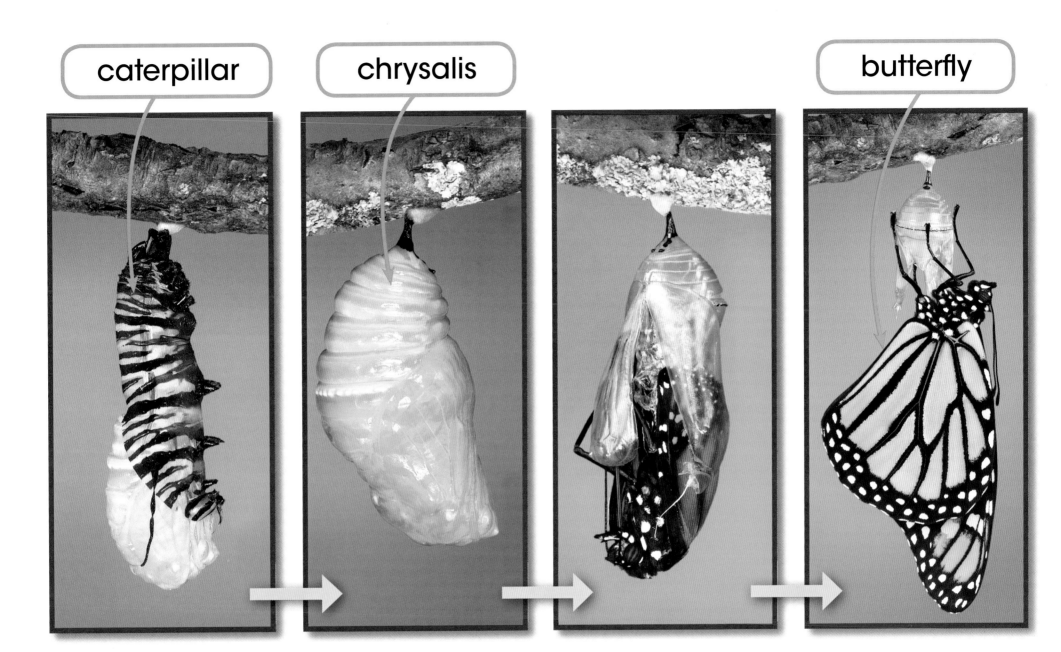

caterpillar

chrysalis

butterfly

Some insects change completely when they turn into adults. A butterfly starts life as a caterpillar. It spins a cover around its body, called a **chrysalis**. Inside the chrysalis it changes into an adult!

17

frog

Another special group of animals are called **amphibians**. Amphibians are animals such as frogs, toads, and newts. They are born in water, but they spend most of their lives on land.

Amphibians lay their eggs in water. The young have **gills** so they can breathe underwater, and tails to help them swim. As they grow, they get **lungs** to breathe in air, and legs for moving on land.

The Human Life Cycle

Humans have life cycles, too. A baby becomes a child. A child becomes a teenager, and then an adult. Adults get older, and eventually they die. When adults have babies, they start the life cycle all over again.

As we grow, our bodies do not change on the outside as much as butterflies or frogs do. Humans take care of their young and teach them new things for much longer than other animals.

How Long Is One Life Cycle?

olive tree

human

sea lion

marigold

hippopotamus

mayfly

How long do you think the living things in the photos might live for?

Answers on page 23

Words to Know

amphibian type of animal that can live in water or on land

chrysalis case around an insect. Inside a chrysalis, an insect changes into an adult.

gills part of an animal's body that helps it to breathe underwater

larva young insect

lung part of an animal's body that helps it to breathe in air

molting growing new skin and losing the old skin

pattern happening in the same order

pollen powder made by plants. Plants reproduce by using pollen.

reproduction to make new life

stage one part or section of a life cycle

Answers to quiz on page 22:
olive tree about 500 to 900 years
human about 70 to 80 years
sea lion about 17 years
marigold about 1 year
hippopotamus about 45 years
mayfly about 30 minutes to 1 day

Index

Note to Parents and Teachers

Before reading

Show the children the front cover of the book. Ask them what they think life cycle means. Explain to the children that a life cycle shows the changes or different stages a living thing goes through in its life.

After reading

- Depending on the time of year, ask each child to create a book about a living thing's life cycle. For example, if it is fall, ask them to make a story about the life cycle of an apple tree. Each page can show one stage of the living thing's life cycle.
- Cut out pictures of different stages of a life cycle. Ask children to order and name the stages. Stick the pictures or photos in the correct order on a display chart.
- As an ongoing class activity, plant a fast-growing seed of a plant that also produces seeds quickly (for example, a bean). Encourage the children to observe the changes and stages of its life cycle week by week.

Pour le petit Ugo

Mes remerciements à Francine

© 2004, l'école des loisirs, Paris
Loi n° 49.956 du 16 juillet 1949 sur les publications
destinées à la jeunesse : mars 2004
Dépôt légal : décembre 2005
Imprimé en France par Imprimerie Clerc
à Saint-Amand-Montrond

Les éditeurs tiennent à remercier M. Gilles Béguin,
conservateur général du musée Cernuschi.

CHEN JIANG HONG

Le cheval magique
de Han Gan

l'école des loisirs
11, rue de Sèvres, Paris 6e

Quand il était petit, Han Gan adorait dessiner.

Mais il ne pouvait s'acheter ni pinceaux, ni papier, car sa famille était trop pauvre.

Afin de gagner un peu d'argent et d'aider ses parents, il travaillait pour l'aubergiste.

Il livrait des repas chez des clients.

Un jour, Han Gan livra un repas
chez le célèbre peintre Wang Wei.

Au moment de repartir, il vit de beaux chevaux derrière la maison,
et ne put s'empêcher de les dessiner sur le sable.
Intrigué, Wang Wei s'approcha et regarda attentivement le dessin.
Puis il dit à Han Gan de revenir le voir le lendemain.

Le lendemain, Wang Wei avait préparé pour Han Gan des papiers,

des couleurs, des pinceaux et un peu d'argent.

« Ceci est pour toi, pour que tu puisses peindre autant que tu voudras… »

Le cœur de Han Gan se gonfla de reconnaissance.

Han Gan dessinait de l'aube au coucher du soleil.
Il aimait par-dessus tout dessiner des chevaux, et toujours il voulait qu'ils aient l'air
le plus vivant possible.

Il était si doué que, quelques années plus tard,
l'Empereur, qui avait beaucoup entendu parler de lui,
le fit venir au palais afin qu'il entre à l'Académie
des peintres officiels.

À l'Académie, Han Gan refusait de s'exercer en imitant les œuvres des Anciens, comme le lui demandait son professeur. Il ne voulait peindre que des chevaux. Et, bizarrement, il les peignait toujours attachés.

« Pourquoi représentes-tu toujours tes chevaux attachés ? » lui demandèrent un jour ses camarades.

Han Gan répondit : « Parce que mes chevaux sont si vivants qu'ils pourraient sortir du papier. »

Alors on commença à raconter
des choses de plus en plus étranges
sur les chevaux de Han Gan…

Quelque temps plus tard, au plus profond d'une nuit silencieuse,

alors que Han Gan travaillait chez lui, un grand guerrier vint le voir.

«Ma visite doit rester secrète», dit le guerrier. «L'ennemi est à nos portes. Je dois partir me battre demain.»

« J'ai entendu dire que tes chevaux
étaient plus vrais que nature, on raconte même
que ton pinceau magique peut les rendre
vivants. Pourrais-tu faire apparaître
pour moi le plus fougueux
et le plus vaillant des coursiers ? »
« Je peux essayer », répondit Han Gan.

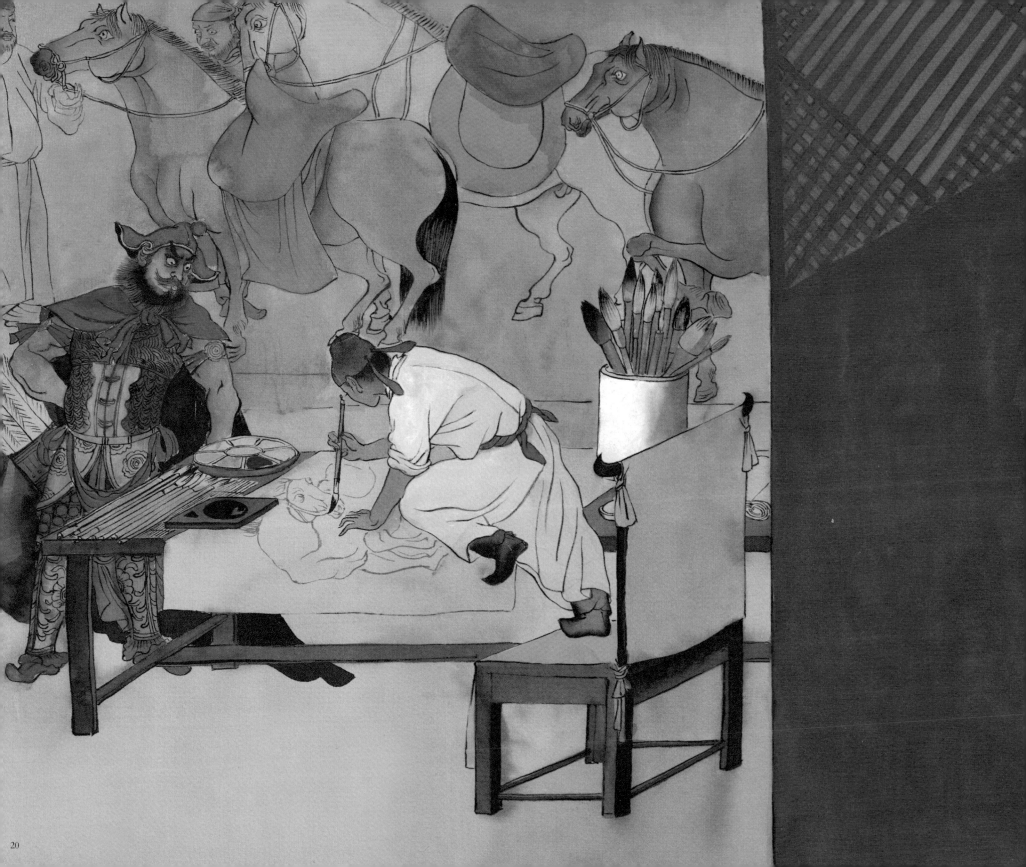

Han Gan se mit à dessiner
avec toute son âme. Mais le cheval
qu'il peignait ne prenait pas vie.
« Continue, il le faut », insista
le guerrier.
« Je suis désolé », dit Han Gan,
« ce dessin ne vaut rien.
Autant le jeter au feu. »

Mais à l'instant
où il jeta le papier,
un fabuleux coursier jaillit
d'entre les flammes.

Ce cheval-là n'avait besoin ni d'eau, ni de fourrage, ni de repos.

Dans son galop, ses sabots
touchaient à peine terre.

Le guerrier, lui,
ne s'était jamais senti
aussi puissant.

Il n'était pas seulement puissant, il était invincible.
Au plus fort du combat, aucune flèche, aucune lance ne l'atteignait jamais.
Ni lui ni sa monture. Le guerrier commença à remporter
de grandes victoires.

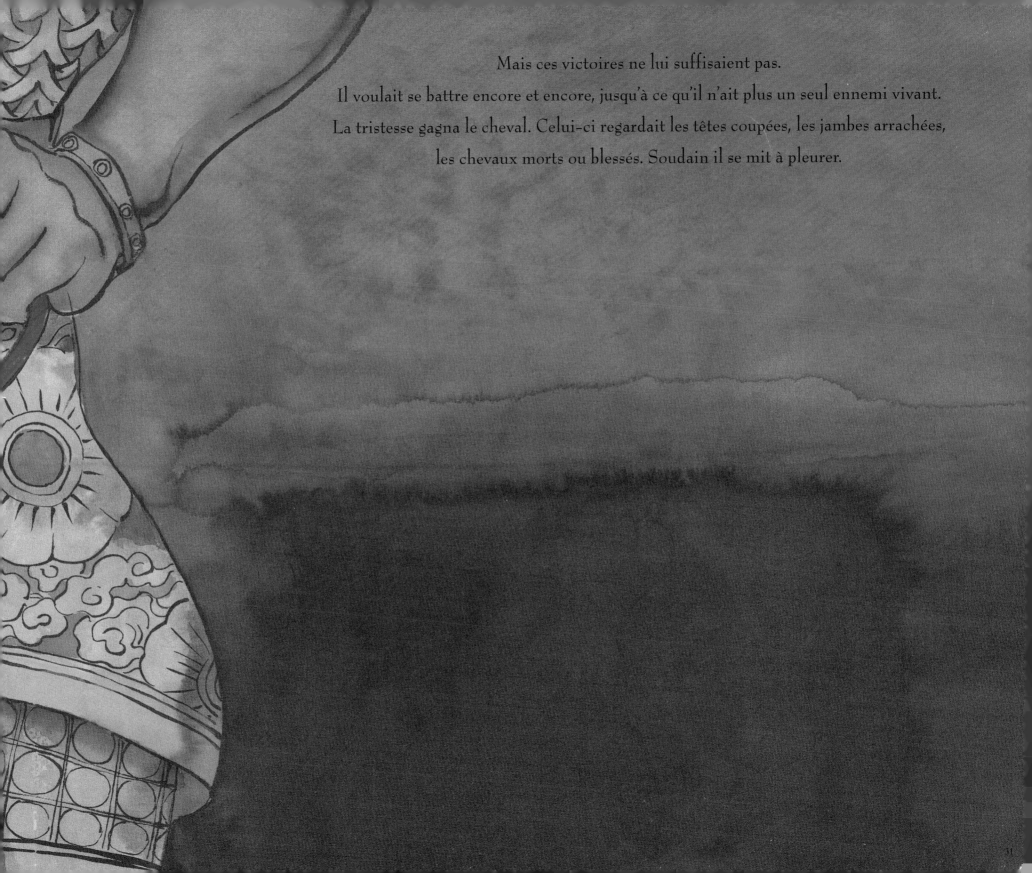

Mais ces victoires ne lui suffisaient pas.

Il voulait se battre encore et encore, jusqu'à ce qu'il n'ait plus un seul ennemi vivant.

La tristesse gagna le cheval. Celui-ci regardait les têtes coupées, les jambes arrachées,

les chevaux morts ou blessés. Soudain il se mit à pleurer.

Se débarrassant du guerrier au milieu du champ de bataille,
le cheval, encore tout couvert de sang, s'élança au grand galop.
Rien ni personne ne pouvait l'arrêter.

Le guerrier chercha désespérément le cheval.

Il le chercha pendant trente-six jours et trente-six nuits.

Un matin d'automne, il arriva devant la maison de Han Gan.

«Ce cheval que tu m'avais donné», dit-il à Han Gan, «il a disparu. Sais-tu où il est?»
«Oui», dit Han Gan. «Tu vois ce tableau? J'y avais peint cinq chevaux. Un matin, quand je me suis réveillé,
il y en avait un sixième. C'est là que ce cheval vit à présent. Dans mon tableau.»

Chevaux et Palefreniers, Han Gan, encre et couleurs sur soie, musée Cernuschi, Paris. © Photothèque des musées de la Ville de Paris, cliché Degrâces.

Le cheval magique est une légende, mais Han Gan a bel et bien existé.

Il vivait en Chine, il y a plus de mille deux cents ans.

C'était un extraordinaire peintre de chevaux.

Ses tableaux frappaient l'imagination, et sa renommée a traversé les siècles.

Il ne reste que très peu de tableaux de lui.

Les illustrations de ce livre ont été peintes sur soie, selon la même technique que celle utilisée par Han Gan.